# When It's Okay to Quit a Job

*101 Acceptable Moments*

Corin Devaso

Copyright © JV 2021

This short book is strictly satire and does not encourage, endorse, or support quitting a job for any reason.

You can also find our fun and effective mindfulness guides by searching for authors Corin Devaso, Harper Daniels, and Logan Tindell on Amazon. Our bestselling mindfulness guide *30 Days to Stop Giving a Shit* can be found on Amazon as well; and as always, we would greatly appreciate reviews so that we can continue writing material. Don't forget to share this book on social media – thank you and enjoy.

30DaysNow.com

**Don't forget to leave a review with your own *"when it's okay to quit a job"* moment!**

## *Before We Begin...*

This fun and short book offers 101 acceptable moments for when it's probably okay to quit a job.

Can you think of another acceptable moment not given in this book? Share it using **#WhenItsOkay**.

Simply post a picture of the book cover on your favorite social media platform, include **#WhenItsOkay**, and tell us your acceptable moment.

By utilizing the hashtag for this series, you can find other interesting insights and stories given by people who are free and independent...or selectively apathetic.

Don't hold back! Tell us your own unique acceptable moment. You just might help someone out or make someone's day.

*Thank you for participating in this book series!*

# It's okay to quit a job...

**1.** When you finally realize that you're not a valued asset.

**2.** If you go into work on your day off and discover your coworkers having a swinger's party.

**3.** When your boss says, "We need to talk tomorrow. I've set up a meeting at 4:30 PM and H.R. will be present."

**4.** If 40-60% of your coworkers are energy vampires.

**5.** Before you're tempted to slap your boss in the face.

**6.** Despite not having an equally, or worse, shitty job lined up.

**7.** If you overhear your boss saying that he or she hates you with a passion.

**8.** If you overhear your boss saying that he or she loves you with a passion.

**9.** When you win the multi-state Powerball.

**10.** After having just started the job and finding out that the company is moving 350 miles away.

**11.** Even though you'll lose money and might go broke.

**12.** If you accidently swipe right on your manager.

**13.** If you have enough emergency savings to get you through the next year.

**14.** If the people closest to you are saying, "You really need to quit that job."

**15.** Before you lose your mind.

**16.** If your heart and gut are telling you to leave.

**17.** After learning to count cards from a poker shark in Reno.

**18.** When your boss says, "Leave on your own, or I'll find a way to fire you."

**19.** When your employer is mentioned in the news for fraud, embezzlement, or racketeering.

**20.** After having driven to work in a state of panic for more than six months.

**21.** If you're consistently being passed up for promotion.

**22.** When everyone is telling you, "Don't do it! Don't quit your job!"

**23.** As soon as you have Wi-Fi, a computer, and a smartphone; so that you can apply for other jobs while unemployed.

**24.** If you daydream often about shitting on your boss's desk or blowing up his or her car.

**25.** If you fantasize a few times a week about a grand exist, such as screaming, "I quit! *(followed by a loud fart)*" in a staff meeting.

**26.** If you work for a for-profit college, Mexican drug cartel, or a presidential administration.

**27.** If you only have a few more days, weeks, or decades to live.

**28.** At any time.

**29.** For mental health reasons, such as overcoming major depression or anxiety.

**30.** If your boss says to the team, "Everyone, I need your attention. This afternoon each of you will be given a drug test. Yes, we are testing for cannabis as well."

**31.** When you are accidentally copied on an email from your boss to his or her friend in H.R. asking about the quickest and easiest way to fire you.

**32.** After a company-wide meeting in which the president announces, "Great news! We are merging with a major corporation!"

**33.** When people are asking you, "Do you still work there?"

**34.** After you ask for a raise, for the twelfth time, and are told no.

**35.** Despite your significant other saying, "If you quit your job to pursue your passion; we are done! This isn't about you, it's about us!"

**36.** Even though you might have to couch-surf around Los Angeles.

**37.** If you have an updated passport and enough money to reach Thailand.

**38.** After having witnessed 87% of your department laid-off within the last year.

**39.** If you wake up every day in a fog of despair, depression, and fear; knowing that your job has something to do with it.

**40.** If the highlight of your day is leaving work.

**41.** If your therapist says, "You've been complaining about your job for three years now. Don't you think it's time to leave?"

**42.** When you would rather drive into a building on the way to work than actually arrive to work.

**43.** If things do not get better within two months.

**44.** After having realized that your boss isn't concerned about your professional growth by any means.

**45.** To pursue your dreams.

**46.** To become the greatest competitor your employer will ever encounter.

**47.** Once you inherit millions of dollars from a long-lost aunt.

**48.** As soon as you start developing severe hemorrhoids and back problems from sitting on your ass all day.

**49.** Before it's too late.

**50.** Even though you're scared shitless.

**51.** If you spend an ample amount of time at work in the bathroom, avoiding the boss or your regular daily tasks.

**52.** If your director announces, "We're sorry, but we can't afford raises this year either. Hopefully next year."

**53.** If your employer doesn't offer good benefits (401K, medical insurance, three weeks of vacation, personal time, sick leave, etc).

**54.** Once you awaken to the realization that you don't need a job, you need a passion.

**55.** After you catch your boss banging the intern.

**56.** If bonuses are awarded as donuts and cookies; and most of your coworkers are experiencing serious health problems as a result.

**57.** If you start weekend binge drinking to escape the reality of your job.

**58.** If you're asked or expected to do something illegal according to state and federal laws.

**59.** If your boss is a micromanaging asshole.

**60.** If you work your ass off, but are not treated with respect.

**61.** After having walked in on your boss snorting lines of cocaine off the intern's thigh.

**62.** Even though there's a voice inside you saying something malicious, such as, "Don't be stupid! Keep the job and suffer through it a while longer. Be unhappy now, for happiness later."

**63.** To try a completely different career field.

**64.** To go back to school (as long as you don't incur a lot of student loan debt).

**65.** To join a crew of assassin ninjas; that assassinates only bad people.

**66.** Before the job quits you.

**67.** After having joined a professional mariachi band.

**68.** Even though you've been promoted.

**69.** When someone kidnaps you, holds you hostage, and says, "I'll let you go if you quit that job."

**70.** If you don't like it.

**71.** After deciding to become a Buddhist Monk or Jesuit Priest.

**72.** If you're visited by an angel or some kind of spiritual being (use your imagination), and it says, "Hey! It's okay to quit your job. You'll be fine."

**73.** As soon as you start dating your boss and/or co-worker(s).

**74.** If you start hearing birds chirping, "Quit your job. Quit your job."

**75.** If you no longer smile or laugh.

**76.** After your boss wrongfully scolds and embarrasses you in front of coworkers, and none of them come to your defense.

**77.** Once you accept that your job is not that important, in the big picture.

**78.** After you break open a fortune cookie and read the fortune "Soon you will make a great decision. Lucky #'s 34 23 68 07 12 06."

**79.** If on the way to your job, every song on the radio has to do with leaving a toxic relationship, making a change, or discovering happiness.

**80.** As soon as you realize that the job you just started has nothing to do with the actual job description.

**81.** If the job is keeping you up at night, staring at the ceiling.

**82.** If you're waking up every night between 2 AM and 4 AM to check the time.

**83.** If it's an obvious dead-end position.

**84.** If you can see yourself 10 years from now, in the same position, with the same employer, stuck and miserable.

**85.** When you realize that the job is taking you from your family and friends.

**86.** If you have the flu or explosive diarrhea, no more remaining sick days, and are expected to go into work regardless of your illness.

**87.** If you hate your life.

**88.** When you no longer find enjoyment in the job, whatsoever.

**89.** When the boss's evil spouse starts coming into work regularly to give people hell; because he or she hates the world.

**90.** If a leprechaun rings your doorbell and says, "Come follow me to the pot of gold!"

**91.** If your direct-superior takes credit for all of your good work and you receive zero recognition.

**92.** If all of your performance evaluations for the last few quarters indicate "Valued Contributor" or "Good Performer"; allowing your employer to give you the bare minimum merit increase.

**93.** Once you are no longer challenged to grow, achieve, learn, and succeed.

**94.** When many of your coworkers are severely sick with contagious diseases because they're scared they'll be fired for taking a sick day.

**95.** Though you might believe you won't find a similar or better position.

**96.** After you've discovered the Stolen Treasure of Montezuma.

**97.** After you've become world-famous for winning the Grand Hot Dog Eating Contest.

**98.** If you find a Rembrandt painting in the attic of an old farmhouse.

**99.** If you fall in love while vacationing in Barcelona.

**100.** If it leads to greater happiness and allows you the time and energy to find your purpose.

**101.** After having read *30 Days to Overcome a Shitty Job*.

*Thank you!*

And don't forget to share your own acceptable moment by using **#WhenItsOkay** on your favorite social media platform.

www.ingramcontent.com/pod-product-compliance
Lightning Source LLC
Chambersburg PA
CBHW031942170526
45157CB00008B/3283